salmonpoetry

Publishing Irish & International

Poetry Since 1981

but don't blink. Another refreshing aspect of the poems is how he salutes his mother, simply and yet with all-consuming empathy. These poems enhance the volatility of change and present us with a tough man not afraid to show his feminine side."

RITA ANN HIGGINS, Poet

"'So now we will form our own words', 'and poetry dispenses with preliminaries'. With Threads Laurence McKeown creates a songline through his incarceration as a 'terrorist' to his recognition as a freedom fighter; through the resilience of his comrades to his rage at their death; through the toll on his family and a 'multitude of unfulfilled desires' until his release into the arms of a lover and his daughters."

OLWEN FOUÉRÉ, Artist and performer

"Many people interested in Northern Ireland's 'Troubles' may well be interested in Laurence McKeown's take on them in this form. I would urge them to spend time with 'Margaret (for my mother)', by far the longest, and (for me) the best poem in the collection. In it the personal and political come together – deftly, unselfconsciously, truly. It is a moving poem – the beating heart of this first book of poems – and worth the price of the whole thing in itself."

DAMIAN GORMAN, Poet and teacher

"I met Laurence more than ten years ago at the Belfast Film Festival, so it was a pleasure to meet him again as a poet. In his poem, 'Red Mick', about a hunger striker who died while they were both in prison, there are a couple of lines which particularly resonate: 'I believe that in the H-Blocks you found something to love and live for / A place to give what was yours to offer.' That's the feeling I had when I finished this book of poems. From it, I was able to understand a little more of what happened to Laurence and how, in the title of another of his poems, he 'learned to speak a new language' – that of poetry. An incredible achievement."

JULIE CHRISTIE, Actress

"I love poetry because I can read it for five minutes or five hours and it will always give something of itself to me. Laurence's collection of poems gave a lot to me. I thoroughly enjoyed reading them and will do so again ... and again. This is poetry of imprisonment, politics, and a touch of erotica. It is very personal, and it is a brave step to share your inner self with the world through publishing. I'm glad he took that step. I suspect that almost everyone in the world has composed at least one poem at some time in their lives. It is an art form available to the masses and the individual. In Laurence's poem 'Introduction' he says that 'poetry dispenses with preliminaries'. Join his conversation; you'll be glad you did."

GERRY KELLY, Political activist

the arts council
an chomhairle ealaíon

funding
literature
artscouncil.ie

THREADS

Laurence McKeown

Published in 2018 by
Salmon Poetry
Cliffs of Moher, County Clare, Ireland
Website: www.salmonpoetry.com
Email: info@salmonpoetry.com

ISBN 978-1-912561-23-0

Cover Artwork: *The author sketched on a street corner in Lagos, Portugal, August 2018,*
              by Attila Bardocz
Cover Design & Typesetting: *Siobhán Hutson*

Printed in Ireland by Sprint Print

Salmon Poetry gratefully acknowledges the support of
The Arts Council / An Chomhairle Ealaíon

Dedicated to all those who have formed the threads of my life

Acknowledgements

There are several people I wish to thank for contributing to this collection of poems. First, those who were the inspiration for many of the poems – be they friend or foe!

The comrades with whom I shared the poetry workshops in the H Blocks of Long Kesh so many years ago – times of laughter, embarrassment, and the occasional tear. But the workshops provided much more than that; they unleashed a creative energy and talent that was later expressed through so many other artistic projects both inside and outside of prison.

That eclectic group of friends and people I admire who I sent the manuscript to before publication for them to read over and offer personal comments, which are included in this publication. To Marian Lovett who read the manuscript and gave me good, timely advice and suggestions for improvement. To Jessie Lendennie (editor of Salmon) who had the good sense to leave some of the shorter poems out. A good decision Jessie! And to Siobhán Hutson who did such a marvellous job with layout and design. To each and every one of you, go raibh míle maith agaibh.

LAURENCE MCKEOWN
November 2018

Contents

Poetry from Prison

Poetry Post Release 1992

Poetry from Prison

Introduction

You said
you knew me
before we met.

I read your thoughts
before you spoke.

Knowledge is social,
comrades, lines of communication,
and poetry dispenses with preliminaries.

Solitary Man

Comrade,
why do you weep unseen?
Why speak fears to yourself
and create echoes of a darker you?

We laugh with one another;
why can't we cry together?

Liberation

The ultimate victory of our struggle
is celebrated daily
in the smile,
work
touch, of a friend.

A Wet Silence

A wet silence.
It hangs about my shoulders,
chilling me to the bone,
and soaks through my pores
diluting flesh in its all-absorbing
stillness.
I am awash in it,
seeing neither land, nor lighthouse,
nor even flotsam upon which to cling
for already my limbs have dissolved,
leaving not a trace nor imprint
to suggest they were once of solid form
and I know now that my lungs
have turned to gills and I'm breathing ..... silence.
A wet silence.

Whose Knowledge; Whose Language?

We thought of it incessantly
and talked long and often
of the words we would read
and the thoughts we would devour
of those we had only of late come to know.

Our hunger knew no bounds,
nor would it be sated
by limitless quantities of a common dish.
Specific ones were read,
then discussed with friends and passed around.
Always they were beneficial
to a more-or-less large degree.

But the hunger was sated
and cretins, we discovered, frequent publishing houses
often in large numbers.

Now I realise we had the literature all along.
It was just that the words were jumbled,
or hidden under the rules we memorized
during our training for life.
It took our captors to reveal them to us;
they who had not been told that before one can speak
one must have a language
and that in this supra-techno world
illiteracy can often mean freedom.

So now we will form our own words
and converse with one another as before
though different now as we are so much younger
in attitude and approach.

I think of putting the splunker in the choo choo for the effort.
A smile parts my lips.
I am back pacing the floor of my cell.

Communication 1

For ages,
our bodies kept apart,
we touched one another with our words.
Written small, but caressingly,
we made love from a distance.

The words,
chosen carefully, thoughtfully,
took the form of lips,
or tongue,
now a hug, a kiss, an embrace;
now two bodies entwined.

And I wondered how literate I was
and if my movements were clumsy.
Did an elbow jar you?
A verb or adjective cause you pain?

It's difficult to affix to paper
an expression,
or write a smile which speaks in silence
words of intensity.

Yet together,
we've shaped over time
fingers from our words,
and our sentences
are as hands which reach out
to hold, to embrace, to touch.

For ages now,
though apart,
we've touched one another with our words,
written small but caressingly.
We've made love from a distance.

Communication 2

Then,
there came a time,
suddenly,
(if tragically)
when words were needless,
cumbersome even,
and letters
confined to history
made way for language of another sort.
And fingers spoke
and hands told tales
of ecstasy,
and of time apart,
and of desires wrapped in plastic,
now rekindled,
now raging with intensity.
And I felt,
as the first human must have felt when
language was discovered.

Good Order and Discipline

They say an inquiry will be held
by the governor and the RUC.
And there's no doubt it will be handled meticulously
and attention will be given to such detail
as the exact time of death
and where precisely they stood, or sat,
those who were 'caring' for him.

And they will inquire as to the type of rope used
and how it was fastened
and who was it found him,
swinging,
or hanging limply, as is a more apt description
of a body that has lost its life
and is dangling at the end of a rope.

And reports will be written
and signatures affixed to the bottom
of countless forms.

On the computer,
his name, age, occupation, and political sympathies
will now be followed with: Died August 11th 1988.
Because the attention they devote to him today
will be no less than that given to him yesterday
when they ensured he had a bed to sleep in
and clothes to wear and food to eat.

And we must be honest and say
that they were attentive to those needs,
just as they were attentive to the pitiless enforcement of
their rules and regulations which demand that
the prisoner will battle for every concession, or privilege,
and that when he is seen to bend, or buckle,
under unknown and untold sorrows

he will have more weight added to his burden,
starved of companionship,
and moved around
so as to be the responsibility
of no one,
so that no one can be blamed
for the inevitable outcome of a process geared
towards
'good order and discipline'.

Persons with names and histories
become bodies with numbers,
become statistics on files.

Robots don't cry – it's much tidier that way.

Mengele

Mengele is alive and well and working in Lisburn.
His 'smile' is easily identifiable to the experienced eye,
the ineptitude of the state sculptor showing quite clearly
in the dead eyes of his creation.
A functionary, a bought person, soul-less,
one who gives a prison-interpretation of clinical.
A man who takes his job seriously
but who forgets what his job is.
Was it once to care for people?
A long time ago; so long ago.

But better not to have such thoughts;
they could be harmful, career-wise.
Better to get on with the job
of treating people and curing their ills.
And some are really badly diseased;
rotten to the core.
So much so that they think themselves healthy
and not only don't ask for treatment
but seek to give advice themselves
and make proposals and suggestions,
criticisms even.

Sands and company were chronic cases of this
disease-infested community
and the virus has not yet been halted
nor even contained.
In fact, it worsens every day
and may even engulf
the province.

Mengele has a job on the frontline.
Mengele is alive and well and working in Lisburn.

Magharaberry (Sir)

A frequent daydream of mine,
in my world of concrete and steel,
is to step on thick green grass and feel it depress,
sponge-like,
beneath my weight.

My wish is not to crush the moss
for the sheer hell of it
but to delight in the sensation
of softness underfoot,
content in the knowledge that with my departure
it will rise again, unperturbed,
to its former position.

I watch a man
walk the tarmacked path
with greenery on either side.
He knows that between the grass and him
rises the impregnable barrier
of his own subservience.

"Stay off the grass," is what would be written,
if it were needed.
But it isn't.

Learning to Speak a New Language

A bit like learning to speak Gaeilge for the first time,
the words stumbling out awkwardly,
not used to hearing them,
at least not publicly anyhow, so direct are they.
A sense of embarrassment even at the sound of my voice
speaking them,
simultaneously looking around at those within earshot.

This awkwardness I feel
provokes the memory of a question once posed in my mind,
"Am I ashamed to speak the language of my people
and let it be known who I identify with and where my roots lie?"

I don't baulk at the question now
because I'm confident
with my reply.
I answer directly in the language of my people,
which is the language of resistance and defiance.
I stand with those who seek freedom, wherever that may be,
and my roots are amongst
"those wretched oppressed whom I am deeply proud to
know as the risen people." (Bobby Sands)

Those who wish to hear me speak
I welcome to my side,
but to others who seek to mock,
belittle, and destroy
that which we have created,
are committed to defend,
and in the future, add to,
I say to them,
"How dare you attempt to silence me
or rob me of my words?
What is this alien language you speak?
Where did it originate
and who brought it here?"

For it is not common in this place.
It is the language of the foreigner,
the language he teaches to his scholars
though he doesn't speak it himself.
Nor do I.

I speak the language
whose words are embedded in the paintwork of these walls
that imprison me.
Their message scribbled shoulder-high,
so tall and erect stood those who wrote them.

This language
will be spoken more clearly soon.
Shakily at first, perhaps,
it will later develop to its full potential.
And it is said that the best way to learn a language
is to live amongst those who speak it
in their work,
and in their actions.

Our community is strong and speaks a common language.
Ours is the language of resistance and defiance.
Ours is the language of revolution.

Across the Sea

Centuries ago,
carrying bibles and guns,
they crossed the sea to us.
And we fought.
If, like you,
they had offered their knowledge and experience
without a price,
we might have become friends.

Feminists

Nicolaus Copernicus, Polish astronomer,
discovered that we don't inhabit an earth-centred universe,
as had been firmly believed before then.

At the time,
he experienced much difficulty in convincing his contemporaries
of the truth of his discovery.

Such theories challenged what was 'natural' and 'God-ordained'
and a disciple of Copernicus
was the worst of heretics.

Four centuries later
we still have our heretics.
Now they're known as feminists.

Margaret

for my mother

I am new to this,
my skill,
if it can be called such,
as yet much flawed.
But I find joy,
not in the purity, or form of completed verse,
but in the release of feelings, thoughts, and ideas
captured in words.

And yet,
therein lies my difficulty,
for with what words will I pen this?
Often when I think of you it's in question form.
Who were you?
As a child, a girl, a teenager?
A fully mature woman?

I knew you as a mother
but there was life before that
of which only you can speak.
So when I write, it is with humility,
capturing only the moments we shared
and not an attempt to say
who, or what, you were
before you became my mother.

My earliest thoughts are of Portrush excursions,
a 'Fr Davy's' annual trip.
Sleepless Friday nights before them, then the joy
of coal ash on my face through an open window
and gasps of fright as darkness came with a tunnel.
I loved the water just as much as Barry's
with its ghost trains and racing cars
and would leave reluctantly only when warned that trains
do not wait for small boys.

On the journey home
I didn't ask you what those boys were doing
with the girl in the next carriage.

The Peeler with white helmet and heavy bike
must have frightened you.
Pursuing a complaint from a mother whose son I'd fought with
but I don't think you took him, or her, seriously.
At least you never said anything to me.

But when Mary Keenan called,
requesting that I refrain from rapping her letter-box
and setting buckets of water at her back door
which her elderly relative stepped into,
as was intended,
I hid from you in shame;
even though I'd thought it funny,
him with his wet feet.
And I still do.

I was 10, 'getting married' and needed new shoes
so you let me go alone to get them,
and I did,
but only after a lengthy argument with John Nutt
who felt sure you'd disagree with my selection;
new 'slip-ons'.
But you didn't.
Most likely you saw the joy on my face and
would endure months of credit
rather than destroy that.

Two years later you waited in silence
while I spun yet another excuse for being home early
from St Malachys,
then showed me a letter from the school

inquiring as to my absence over a 3-week period.
You cried
as my Da raged
but to you, knowledge was not measured in paper diplomas
nor should the price of it be happiness.

You pretended not to notice how the
gold bands on the cigarette packets
(My Da bought for visitors at Christmas)
had become ragged and torn.
Instead, you turned your back each morning
while I grabbed two, or three, for school.

And the morning you barely spoke to me,
clearly the memory still vivid of me on my knees
just a few hours previously
inserting a key into a doorstep instead of a lock
and the smell of brandy, wine, and beer
you felt inappropriate for classrooms.
However,
by evening it was forgotten,
for you were more interested in the present
than in the past
and more inclined towards embracing
than holding others at arms length.

I left hurriedly one night in '74
without goodbyes.
No doubt it was a shock to you
though I wonder?
For you knew me so well
and soon inquiries led you
across the border.
But hotels are for lovers to meet in
and our expressions had to speak
the words we never uttered.

You looked so vulnerable that day
in the world of Diplock (courts);
tired and sad, with an air of inevitability.
I longed to go to you and hold you
but the metal encasing my wrists held me to another.
Stripped of the rhetoric
our struggle was exemplified in that scene of
the assembled might of Imperialist power
aligned against one woman
who stood before them and said, "He's my son."

On the visits,
tension shaped your features
and your eyes asked questions about the food
and the search I would get upon my return.
Local events were described in great detail,
accompanied with a list of well-wishers and
the customary comment on how well I looked
(such a lie God would easily forgive).
Then,
attentive eyes momentarily distracted,
you passed to me the gift you'd carried as close to you
as once you'd carried me
and in that act, love conquered fear,
as it always does.

In '81 you covered many miles on my behalf,
walked many roads,
shook many hands,
until the day the struggle was brought direct to you.
"You know what you've to do and I know what I've to do."
you whispered at my bedside;
the resolution of two conflicting possibilities
left in the hand of fate.
Then you went off to kneel and pray amidst your tears.

When next we met,
the scars of that battle were etched deeply upon your face.
Hustled in and out again
we got no chance to say the things we wanted to
and I wondered
if you'd left still unsure
of how I felt
towards you.
You who were blameless.

The happiest I ever saw you
was on your return from the States a year later;
a life-long dream fulfilled in the act of placing flowers
on your father's grave.
And the joy you experienced in your newly-discovered fame
as the mother of a freedom fighter
not a terrorist.
Concerts stopping mid-way through to introduce you to the
audience who
rose and applauded.
You leaned across to me and whispered, conspiratorially,
of how you met a woman you believed to be a socialist,
and I smiled at your earnestness.

When last I saw your face
I raged at the irony of it all.
I was
where you longed for me to be,
at home,
but there
only on account
that you were no longer present.
And later that day we buried you.

Life has moved on since then
and there's so much I'd like to tell you.
The things I've learnt

about myself and others
and how we go on with life
together.
How I've realised that we must tell those we love
of that love for them
in case it's just not obvious.

And I'd like to hear you now
telling of the joys, the pleasures, and passion
of sex outside of marriage
(you were pregnant with Mary when you married)
instead of the pain society can inflict.
I'd kiss and hug you
for being so real and human and loving.
For being a woman
never mind about certificates.

If you'd confess to pranks at school,
of stealing apples from an orchard,
or money from your mother's purse,
we would laugh together
in the knowledge that you knew of every penny I'd taken.

But I don't know your story
Mary Margaret O'Hagan.
I cannot speak your life;
that was yours to tell.
I can but snatch images of you and
say what those meant to me.
I'd like to think though, that if you read this
you'd laugh in places
and cry in others.
Just as I did while writing it.

Goodnight Margaret.

Chained

for my father

You would probably have raged at me Dad;
just another example of how I couldn't care less you'd say.
In reversed roles you would have accepted what was on offer
and tipped your cap to the Sirs.

But then Dad that's how we saw life; differently.
You grew up in a world which taught you that
even if life was tough you were better off than others
and should be content with that.

But those were only some of the chains they bound you with.
There were others more tightly pulled and therefore much closer
to your chest and heart and lungs, and their coldness
suffocated the warmth in you.

In many vests and jerseys they swaddled you; from the cold they said
and though you must often have felt the heat of
pent-up emotions, of love, and pride, and longing
you never knew how to undress.

I can rage at those who made you that way.
They doubtless revelled at their creation and
their successors greeted you with a knowing look
of a master to his slave.

So I was happy when I saw you at rest and smiling.
No doubt that was the undertaker's professional touch,
though I prefer to think of it as the last living expression
of a man finding his freedom.

I know that beneath the cloth and shroud
rested hands, hard, calloused, yet gentle.
The honest hands of a slave who never knew
that he could be master.

I meant to steal a glance at Paddy that day
and no doubt he would reply, if spoken to,
that you may have ignored his kegs for a while
but you couldn't avoid his teak.

And being you, you'd laugh at that
and toss your head back and utter to those around
that that Marrion's one 'fly bastard'
and they would do well to remember that.

But Dad, I'm thankful I'm not like you
and that I've learnt how to undress.
In fact it's something I'm growing to delight in
sun-bathing in the nude.

And the sun, I've found, shines often.
It can appear at night or in a darkened room
and its heat is best felt when temperatures
are well below freezing.

But it is we who let it shine from within us
allowing it to radiate out through the chains
so that soon they don't hold so tight;
soon they melt and fall away.

So I'm glad for you that the chains are off
and yet I rage at those who dared to bind you
and at the others who would beat their breasts in prayer,
then pay the jailer.

All the thoughts have gone now, of emigration,
of landscaping at the cross-roads, of golf courses and hotels,
of ice-cream parlours, hot-dog stands, and veg production;
dreams of adult childhood.

And yet the dreams became meaningless years ago
because they weren't just there for you, but for her also.
Did you not realise that the dreams she wanted most
you held within you?

You had the power to make them real
to breathe life into them and give them body
because all that was required was to speak them out
and they would come alive.

Because happiness is not found in concrete and wood
but in the words we speak to those we love
and the smile we bring to their face when we say, "I need you,"
is the dream come true.

What use is there being able to stand erect
if we cannot shamelessly embrace those we love?
And of what use to us is language if
we do not speak?

So, Dad, I will forget your life as a slave,
allow the silence to remain where you did not speak,
and instead recall the fleeting smile of a now free man
unashamedly naked.

Camillo

I wasn't lost, nor was I crawling on all fours,
but envisaging my destination did not mean knowledge of the route
and my limbs didn't yet possess the strength
to hold me erect in stormy weather.

But I was eager to grow strong and knowing my destination
I sought for the path that would
take me there in the shortest time possible and which
would be bereft of potholes.

We met then, you from a different world,
and we laughed at your childhood heroes and adult perceptions
while you showed me, by example, that teachers are also students
and that study means conflict, means change.

You taught me that the strong are often so because they
know their weaknesses
and that the shortest route is not always the best.
On winding roads we can encounter fellow-travellers
and come alive to the scenery of our lives.

The storms have been frequent since then
but your lessons in posture and position have helped me
to ride with them when they gust, to advance when they wane,
and to utilise their strength to my advantage.

I've wondered during the course of my travel
if my destination is yours also
because even if we both take different routes
our goal can be the same.

And if that journey's end is the summit of the 'new man'
there too must be the 'new woman'
who knows of winding roads and the weaknesses of the strong
and who can laugh at childhood heroes and adult perceptions.

Suspended Time

The light was soft and cast long shadows
across your cheek and brow.
I felt your hand move to caress
and reassure me of your presence.
Tracey (Chapman) spoke loudly to us,
confirming our suspicions that certainty
is but for a moment
and time not deterministic.
Because we were having our future in that moment.

Nature

Despite a conscious effort to control it
my heart beat rapidly
when told that my father's had
stopped.

Cling Film

Cling film was manufactured to preserve
that which was slowly decaying.
Who could have foreseen
that it would one day encase
that which is growing
and becoming stronger daily?

Janet

The crater
in the floor of your kitchen,
in contrast to your diminutive figure,
appeared enormous.
It was the centre of attention.

But looking again at the picture
I realise that
the hole is empty,
useless to humankind,
arrogant and intrusive,
just like the politics of its creators
(British soldiers).
And you,
tower above it,
alive, resilient, dignified,
and tomorrow you will walk
defiantly
where the crater once was.

In the shanty towns of South Africa
you are called Winnie.
In the back streets of Belfast
you are known as Janet.

Indecisiveness

Did you ever stand on the edge of a cliff
and look over
to the rocks below
at the ground
indistinct from that angle and height?

After a time
the cliff face becomes your 'ground',
the ground, a cliff,
or wall,
in the distance
and its only as you lean over that bit more,
then feel the change of gravity
pull on your body,
that you realise
(to your horror)
that you have leaned over too far
and feelings of remorse, regret, stupidity
overwhelm you.

A desire to wind back time engulfs you
and as the air rushes past, you think
why the fuck did I ever want to look over a cliff edge?

In Darkness

Huddled in soft darkness
his dry sobs send coal dust swirling.
Outside, a predator stalks fresh prey;
cocky, confident in his power.
Male power.
Abuse of power.

Flesh-hard male strength
pierces adolescent softness and
batters a mind.

Today,
a cigarette glow illuminates
silent tears.
A young man lives on in the soft darkness
of a coal bunker.

Hard Lines

Right angles and straight lines;
they're everywhere.
And I don't like their rigidity.
Wall, ceiling, floor;
straight, sharp, cold, clinically-exact lines
meeting in
right angles.

The window has 20
right angles and straight lines.
The door 4
(8 if we count the spy-hole),
the grille 120.
I've counted them.

The canteen is full of them;
tables, shelves, and
benches of straight lines and
right angles.

Well, I want twisted, crooked lines.
Winding, curling, meandering paths,
slopes, mounds, hollows, peaks, valleys, dips,
curves,
of land and flesh.

And I want them coloured;
purples, blues, greens, yellows,
bright reds.
No more black and white, or
grey uncertainty.

And in different textures too please
if you don't mind.
No more choice of rough, or
very rough.
How about fine, soft, furry, fluffy, smooth?
Satin, silk?

Robotic minds, administrators, bureaucrats,
created this world of geometric precision.
Did they think it beneath themselves
to apply their engineering skills to the humble
toilet bowl?
The only work of prison art and anarchy.

Vulnerability

Fix your eyes upon me
naked,
vulnerable to a blow.

Circle round me,
look for traps.
There are none.

Interrogate me,
question my motives.
I will answer truthfully.

Cut me.
Watch blood ooze from
armour-less flesh.

Hit me.
See white turn to
blue, black, and
yellow.

When you are sure
I pose you no risk,
come to me
unclothed.

Fix your eyes upon my vulnerability;
protect me.

Encircle me with your arms;
hold me.

Let your eyes question me.
Mine will reply.

With your tongue,
pierce my lips.
Bruise me in passion.

Take me into your warmth.
Feel complete, or
complemented, but never
displaced.

The Rang

Scattered mumblings in early evening.
Tentative steps,
though possibly appearing
sure-footed.
Rigid, nervous positions causing backache
But,
appropriate for formal identification.
Later, laughs .... and redners,
combined with soul-searching debate.

The steps are steep
but with each one our load gets lighter.

And we're being helped along the way.
Thank you.

Dawn

At 4.00 a.m., or just after,
the sky lightened as dawn broke through razor wire.

Face against the bars,
sleepy eyes gazed out on a rigid calm.
Sharp, crisp air invaded the nostrils and
lips puckered in a smile at the thought of a beach.
Beauty and freedom.

Daydreams ended abruptly;
severed by shouts of
'wing search'.

Discontented Husband

Thug.
Yes, you.
I see through your façade.
That elegant blouse clings to a breast
that holds no heart.
Those shapely legs in fashionable culottes
power stiletto heels into
my brain.

Yes, you,
Thug.
Your carefully coloured lips smile
for others but
mouth jagged words to me.
Painted eyelashes meet in a gesture of disdain.
I'm dismissed
with a toss of auburn locks
a flick of manicured hand.

Thug,
tattoo your knuckles,
shave your head,
wear Bovvers,
chew gum.
That way we'll recognise you,
and avoid you.

And by the way,
Thug,
the dishes still aren't done.

An Event

We didn't train today.
We usually do,
three times a week
Tuesday, Thursday, Saturday;
Joe, Tommy, Cypie and me.
It was a break from routine,
different from other Saturday mornings.
It was an event.
We didn't train today.

The Deity

Trademark-studded athletic garb,
as yet unconvinced,
walked circles of its own shadow.
Talk was of forecasts,
often detailed, long and short range,
always the obligatory touch
of cynicism.

Gradually others appeared,
men who hungered after the gold,
knowing no limits to
their worship of the Deity.

They weaved their way
lazily but deliberately through
the light throng of infidels,
on towards the hallowed ground.

There they laid mats, knelt a moment,
stripped naked, then prostrated themselves,
spread-eagled,
before their God(dess).

She blinked through lingering cloud,
smiled lovingly upon the faithful,
then bathed them in her glow.

Frustration

Open the grille please.
No.
Look, I'm dying to go to the bogs.
No.
It's after two o'clock.
No.
Come on ahead.
No.
Why not?
Not allowed to.
Look we should be unlocked by now anyway.
Not yet.
What do you mean, 'not yet'?
Not until we get word.
Come on ahead. I'm really bursting here.
No.
Sure you know everyone's here, you just did a count.
Doesn't matter.
Look, will you open this fucken grille?
No.
Are you a fucken robot or something?
No.
Then open this grille.
Not until I get word.
You're one bastard you know that.
No.
Aye, just obeying orders, is right, obeying fucken orders, aye.

Close Up

Do you know the feeling when you're
just out of bed and you
haven't yet eaten breakfast or even
drank some tea and
he walks up to you,
all considerate like, and asks,
'Did you hear that scéal yet?'
And it just hits you and
you turn away and
mumble something indistinct but
he follows you,
conscientiously carrying out his duty to
inform a comrade,
to keep him abreast of current affairs,
up to date with the political situation in the country,
or the latest air, rail, or boat disaster,
and he just doesn't realise because
no one has ever told him and
you don't have the nerve yourself to say,
"Phew, your breath stinks!"

For the remainder of the day
you avoid him and converse with colleagues
at a distance of several feet whilst
occasionally blowing into your cupped hands
and sniffing quickly;
just in case!

Governor

It was years since we'd last met
but I recognised him immediately.
Possibly it was where he sat,
in a 'position of power',
or just the occasion,
but it helped put name to rank.

He spoke softly, a mild-mannered man this.
He smiled,
honestly I'm sure,
and said,
in his own soft-spoken, mild-mannered way,
"Retribution; not enough of it yet in your case."

Mary

for my sister

To an anxious child,
your pleated skirt offered
protection and security.

It's cloth covered
the maturing curves of
prepubescent maternalism,
and, moistened with my tears,
provided warmth and comfort.

Today, in adulthood I
feel fortified by your strength,
nourished with your love.

I don't run along behind you any more,
but if ever you need me,
just look over your shoulder.
You'll find a child
tugging at your pleats.

Tom

for Tom McElwee who died on hunger strike

He was sitting up in bed
with a cigarette between his lips.
It was the morning of
the day the sun shone.

His voice was weak, but clear,
his one eye sharp in focus,
and he smiled over at me.
That morning of
the day the sun shone.

At noon from the radio
I learnt he had died.
I remember it clearly.
It was the day the sun shone.

Freedom's Wall

You got 25
chips,
I got 5.
We shared them evenly; 15 each.
There was no wall then.
Now it's ever-present when we meet
and especially
when we part.

Bottled Up

Whatever about its after-taste,
vomiting clears the system.
Not so the cancer of repressed conflict.

Without Verbs

Closed doors on a silent wing,
breakfast-time minus breakfast,
rumours colliding with unusual sounds,
unanswered questions withering
on the lips of the agitated.
Frustration, impatience, impotence
good day Friday.

A Poem

She spoke calmly but resolutely.
I listened,
moved by her warmth,
touched by her simplicity.
And in the silence that followed
it seemed as if the very air stood still.

It's History

Easter Monday 1916
is history,
if often now a revised one.

We commemorate it,
a few recall it,
some claim it as their own,
others pretend it never happened.
But it's history.

Such a day
had been dreamed of by a few,
spoken of by fewer,
planned by a minority.

Their firepower?
The outrageous thought that the lowly
could make history.

Easter Monday 1916
is history
because it was made to happen.

Red Mick

for Mickey Devine who died on hunger strike

The day I first met you,
(to speak to that is),
you were slowly dying.
Not something which was immediately noticeable on your face
but then you had only begun to die and
that was why we were together in that room
because some thought they could stop that death;
stop it by appealing to those they saw as the
weaker element in the fight.

Two days later we realized they consisted of
a small degree of sincerity,
a large amount of naivety, and
their loyalty was to political and ecclesiastical masters
rather than to the dying.

They will have taken away with them an image of you,
distinguishable features most likely,
just as others who knew you will define you in various ways.
As the child born on 20/5/54, who
grew up in Springtown and then the Bog,
brother of Margaret,
husband of Maggie,
father of Mickey Junior and Louise,
friend of Noel,
and associate of Eamonn.
Each will have their own story to tell.

But it was many years later that I read these details of your life
for they were unimportant at the time we first met,
our world being very much of the present and possible future
and reminiscences were for later when sleep would not come.

Your end was not glorious,
not as heroes die in Hollywood creations,
and in Ten Men Dead someone comments that really
you had very little to live for.

I dispute that,
though I understand that it was spoken from another's world.
For I believe that in the H Blocks you found something to
love and live for,
a place to give what was yours to offer
and not be judged by societal norms,
exalting the few and damning the multitude.
And you loved and lived that so much
that you loved and lived it
to death.

Prisoners

They can radiate happiness in play, or
reflect peace of mind in their stillness.
Occasionally, sadness clouds them,
tears well up, and
their light flickers, dims,
until rekindled by resilience.

Poetry Post Release, 1992

Oiléan Toraigh

An Gaeilge le cluinstin,
Maighdean Mara,
bosca ceoil,
agus an bád in ám.

Media Heroes

He was a hero,
the judge,
the media,
and his handlers proclaimed.

Nelson (not Lord)
saved 217 lives
they said.
But he killed two
innocent taigs
(that's with a small 't')

The other,
the RUC man,
killed 3,
in the Sinn Fein centre.
"A hero under stress,"
they said.

Árainn Mhór

On Árainn Mhór
I paused before uttering the word,
mainland.

Work

Working?
nawh…
still on the dole.
Doing bits and pieces about the house though.
You know,
a bit of renovation.
Put central heating in,
new kitchen,
new living room,
new hallway,
new bathroom.
Put new windows in; double glazing.
New doors also.
Did all the woodwork and tiling myself.
Painted and decorated the place.
Made a lawn, front and back.
Planted trees, Castlewellan Golds;
twenty-eight of them.
Converted the attic into a study.
Published a book.
Finished my degree.
Started a doctoral thesis, by research.
Wrote a poem
and a film script.
Nawh…
I'm not working.
I'm still on the dole.

Partisans

Was it worth it?
asks the woman
in Italy.
The deaths,
all 10 of them
in prison?

Ask your parents,
the partisans.

Rule Britannia

The words,
"Certainly not",
have a particular ring to them.
They're the type of words you spit out,
especially with emphasis on the
not.

I heard them the other day on the TV
spoken with a cultured English accent.

They were uttered,
not in anger,
not even with passion,
but in disdain.
Pronounced in a very definitive manner
in response to the question
"Would you apologise to the O'Reilly family
for the murder of their daughter Karen?"

Words to the Therapist

Grief in others,
you can talk at great lengths about.
Why not just one word
about the grief that's mine?

Jan '04

A weak sun shines through my window,
shrubs shake in the strong icy wind,
and I think of you, my love.

I see you in all the simple things,
the cup you held,
the carpet you walked upon,
the mirror that held your gaze,
the bed where we made love.

I think of you, my love,
as I type these words from a space
that is yours as well.
I think of you,
my love.

A Rope Bridge

A rope bridge
sways in the wind,
it's hemp wet and slippery,
timbers missing,
others rotten,
unseen,
until they break underfoot.

But with each step
our past recedes
and a new vista nears
with the promise
of becoming sure-footed
on solid ground.

And when we reach it,
we look back at the bridge
connecting two peaks
and suddenly our fears
have vanished, or at least
seem so much smaller.
Now the bridge looks helpful;
a connection between
two stages in a journey.
A friend, not an enemy.

I Awoke This Morning

I'm aching for you.
Since early morning I've been
aching for you.

Was it your talk of longing,
a nightmare slowly receding,
thoughts of you arriving soon,
or memories of days already spent?

Images of you crowd my thoughts,
naked,
on a bed,
hair fallen around your shoulders,
your eyes, your face, your breasts
your navel.

I rest my face on it
as my hand strokes
your thigh.

I've been here before,
at this place,
in time and
space.

Paradise
is before me.

Kids Talk

Daddy,
I'm not saying your house isn't nice;
it is.
But you see being one night at Mammy's
and then to your house
and then to Mammy's and
back and forward and
back and forward...
I'm getting tired.
Could we not just stay at our house with you and Mammy?

But Caoilfhionn
that wouldn't be fair on Daddy.

I'm not saying Órlaith that I don't like daddy's house;
it's just that one house would be better.
That's all I'm saying.

Roverto 2003

Cold water from the mountain river
splashes over the dam and
flows under the bridge.
Cars intrude upon the cobbled streets,
teasing their way like anxious visitors.
Graffiti, scrawled under archways,
proclaims an end to fascism.
Colourful striped flags demanding 'PACE'
hang lifeless alongside beautiful window boxes.
A couple appear at a balcony on the first floor.
His arm reaches out
to touch the flag and
rearrange its folds like a young girl's frock.
Her arm
encircles his waist from behind and
pulls him back indoors.
A man cycles past,
leaning into the pedals and the steep hill
while his infant male passenger
sprawls in his carrier.
Old women dressed in black
carry fresh bread rolls home for breakfast.
The town is lazy in the early morning.
Its inhabitants respect silence.

In Adoration

In boyhood he knelt,
rosary in hand,
and fingered the beads.

Hail Mary full of Grace
the Lord is with Thee.

In manhood he still prays
on his knees
at the foot of his bed
fingering a lace thong,
worshipping yoni.

Bogota, Columbia

Battered cars and trucks,
too many or too close,
vibrate the hotel walls
in downtown Bogota.

Between cotton sheets I lie awake
in plush accommodation,
body clock at home in Ireland
at the breakfast table.

Hotel sounds are much the same
the world over.
Like prison sounds
they echo the lives of captured humanity.

Black Triangle

In black and white films
smelling salts were held to the nostrils of the unconscious
to revive them.
So too
your black, silk pants
taken from the laundry basket
stirred me.

In Tucson

I think of you
toiling in Tucson under an Arizona sun,
uprooting, to nourish new growth
across an ocean.

I picture you,
moist skin glistening,
body taut as you push and pull,
lift and carry, scrape and clean.

I long for you
as you undress to shower,
water caressing curves
I ache to touch.

The Altean Beach

A 'poop-trail' runs from
promenade to pebbled beach,
littered with droppings
from cat, dog, and mountain goat.
But it is shorter
than the route through the estate
of private villas
with pools and burglar alarms.

The uneven stones
that form the Altean beach
make lying on it
very uncomfortable,
unless you take time
to rearrange the pebbles,
sorting large from small
and casting aside debris.

They also make it
awkward getting in and out
of the water to swim,
or when you need to pee.

A goat herder walked his flock.
Bells tinkled as they trod their path.
A woman with drooping breasts,
her step slow and unsteady on the pebbles,
gazed over.
A jet ski roared past
too close to shore.

My fingers gripped your pants;
you moved ever so slightly,
by way of assent,
and to facilitate their removal.

I leaned forward and kissed
your neck.

Oil Painting

Painted on canvas stretched on a bone frame,
natural oils and sweat giving shape and contour;
you posed, almost lifeless.

Big Doc

for Kieran Doherty who died on hunger strike

As teenagers new to prison
your striking good looks were envied,
your physique admired,
your confident step
something we could never imitate.

In that strange and hostile world
your physical presence gave us security,
yet you were little more than a boy yourself,
grown to manhood rapidly.

A short life,
as schoolboy internee,
or on active service with Óglaigh na hÉireann,
gave weight to your words
though few words you spoke.

Your smile gave encouragement,
a nod of your head
enough to prompt compliance.
Even those who incarcerated you
admired you, wanted to be like you
in their dream-world.

When I last saw you,
in the prison hospital in '81,
only the shell of your body remained.
Your movements slower, though just as definite,
your eyes, clear as ever,
and your voice, soft as before,
confident, assured, steady,
"Lean ar aghaidh."

In Your World

I'd like to see you in your world,
walking on scorched earth
lit by the beam of a torch,
alert to rattlers and their colleagues;
snakes of a different kind.

The cry of coyotes in the night,
the smell of horses,
the bald-headed eagle,
cacti and mountains.
Mexican food, salsa, tortillas,
cowboys in their finery.

A mother who reared you,
those who befriended you,
with stories about you
to thrill and embarrass.

To watch dark clouds gather
in the afternoon,
then listen to the rain fall
as we make love
together
for the first time
in your world.

1981

On 10 days they died,
but for 217 they lived,
hoping to halt the 10
days of their deaths
in 1981.

5 years for 5 demands,
then 7 fasting for 53 days
in 1980.

Their fate in the hands of others,
their lives, their own
to decide,
in 1981.

21st Century Witch

She was a witch;
could put grown men to sleep,
even jailors.
The prisoners broke free,
seized government,
became ministers,
closed the jails, and
made new laws.

The witch,
became a judge;
respectable, almost.
But former captives
still look on her as a witch
who can put grown men to sleep.

Afters

The medium-cooked fillet mignon
parted easily
under the serrated edge of his knife.
Juices dripped as he fed forkfuls to his mouth.

Across the table,
her flesh anticipated a similar separation
under the moist firmness
of his tongue.

Whatever Happened to Postcards?

At the Marriott Hotel resort, proper dress code is in place,
except for the young girl close by the grill bar
who bares her breasts,
then looks around to see if someone will look her way.
Her friend jumps with glee at the sound of the latest
downloadable ring tone
coming from her huge, leather (and totally impractical) beach bag.
"Hi mum, yes, having a lovely time. Yes, sun is shining.
We're here on the beach. Lucy's just done her nails.
I'm going for a pee soon. Love to you all.
See you when we get home."

Buddhism

You should practice Buddhism,
be patient,
allow others their process,
don't shout or scream,
let situations evolve,
hold your tongue,
listen, observe,
make eye contact,
relax your jaw.

You should practice Buddhism;
then I wouldn't have to.

Empirical Prices

In the Metro,
latest supermarket chain to arrive in Sharm El Sheikh,
we feel secure with English labels,
prices clearly marked,
and a fully-itemised receipt;
can't be ripped off that way.
Not like the local store,
Egyptian-owned,
where the fruit and veg is unwashed,
they haven't heard of McVities,
and can barely speak 'please' and 'thank you'.
But I leave with a full basket and a fatter wallet.

On the Promenade

No, I don't want to read an English paper
and definitely not the Sun, or Daily Mail.
No, no, no, no, no.
And by the way,
I'm Irish, not English.
Don't add insult to annoyance.

Motion Passed

At the Annual General Meeting of the
Association of Scientific Studies into Enlightened Systems
delegates passed a heavily-amended motion
aimed at reducing global hunger, poverty, and disease.
The outcome of their lengthy deliberations
was about as useful as
the motion I passed this morning
shortly after breakfast.

Albufeira

At home, after dinner
we often have chocolate
with grapes, or maybe strawberries;
sometimes crackers and cheese.

In Albufeira,
after dinner,
beside the open street windows,
at the end of the table,
on the chequered cloth,
by way of dessert,
you spread before me
a moist offering
you had not bought earlier
in the hypermarket.

Many Uses

Ten years after the Good Friday Agreement,
which supposedly heralded an end to war,
explosions are once again heard in South Armagh.

Strangely, politicians don't rush to condemn,
security forces seem uninterested;
even the media is quiet.

With the exception of AA Roadwatch,
who announce the time of the explosions
and advise alternative routes.

Dynamite can tear down the old,
or help construct the new
(bypass).

Corners Caucasus

Corners Caucasus was water;
from the skies over Hopa,
on the windscreen,
in the fish farms,
in the waterfall,
in the Black Sea.

Corners Caucasus was water.

Was water
that we drank from bottles,
never from a tap,
and with gas.

Water,
with its nourishing minerals
in Tskaltubo,
where Stalin had his tub.

Corners Caucasus was water.

Was water,
in the fountains in Baku
by the Caspian Sea.

Water.
Water.

Corners Caucasus was water.

In the streets of Batumi,
in the streets of Batumi,
everywhere in the streets of Batumi.

Corners Caucasus was water.

Was water
was water.

But water is life,
is needed for life to start
and for life to continue.
No enzymes work in the absence of water.
No other liquid can replace water.
Our bodies are over 70% water,
so too is the Earth.
Water = life.
I know: I once survived for 70 days on water alone.

Life,
with Biryasam in Hopa,
working for a better life
but not forgetting the music.

Life,
in Baku, where young couples embrace affectionately,
challenging claims of Muslim conservatism.

Life,
in Tskaltubo
for the refugees displaced by conflict.
And for the locals whose lives also changed
with the collapse of an Empire.

Life,
in the market in Telavi,
in its people,
or in its death form, on offer at the stalls.

Life,
of the children of Ciyni,
who giggle at the visitors from afar,
then display their skills in dance.

Life,
and relics of previous lives
unearthed by MIRAS in Azerbaijan.
Life.

Corners Caucasus was water.
Water is life.
Corners Caucasus was life
at the corners.

The Lost Crown of Croatia

At Jasenovac,
site of a World War II concentration camp,
on the first day of Balkans Xpedition,
I lost my crown.
Not the type that royalty wear,
but a tooth.
It happened during lunch,
itself an incongruity,
given the place
where we sat
with our picnic
on a sunny day.
It was a front tooth,
prominent,
noticeable by its absence,
and vanity,
vanity
engulfed me.
First day of Xpedition,
14 more to go,
self-image,
vanity.
A lost crown
at a place
where many would have offered
mouthfuls of teeth,
a limb,
an orifice,
anything,
to escape their fate.
Such thoughts
banished vanity.
The green fields at Jasenovac
cover corpses,
thousands of them,

tens of thousands,
but in the sunshine
and landscaped earth
they create a serenity,
a stillness,
an awareness of the past
and what happened
in a way that gravestones could never achieve.
I did see gravestones,
on Xpedition Balkans,
in city parks
where children should play,
or older people sit and chat.
But there's no space for that now;
the dead have displaced the living.
We talked about the dead at Jasenovac.
They had names
in a book
and photos too.
We didn't hear the names of others,
more recently killed,
in other cities
in conflict.
The bullet-marked walls screamed
"SILENCE."

Women

It was a woman,
Mary Margaret,
who carried me until birth.

Others later joined her,
to carry me
through life.

May it also be women
who provide me
with the last lift.

Move Over

She heard it in the distance,
almost inaudible at first,
but definite, nonetheless.

Had others heard it?
Obviously not; their inane chatter continued;
house prices, university fees, health insurance.

She followed the sound,
knowing the roads it manoeuvred,
the bends it took,
the potholes it avoided.

She knew how long it would take
to meet it;
to meet him.

She had by now timed it to perfection,
the short path from the back lawn,
past the all-weather tennis court,
to the hump-backed bridge below
where she would stand beside the great oak tree.

The distinctive putt-putt-putt of the Harley
suddenly increased in volume.
She could sense him change gears
and open the throttle.

"Is that a lawnmower?" Julie inquired.
"If it is, they need a new one." Barry laughed.
And the conversation went back to
the social impact of immigration
and the implications of Brexit.

She followed the sound
as it faded into the distance,
felt herself sway with each bend it took,
felt the throbbing energy between her thighs;
felt good.

He was a devil; an adorable devil.
He knew they had guests tonight.

Birth

Filled with
absolute certainty.
Never a shadow of doubt,
until that instant,
when the doctor's surgical gloves
moved across her belly.
What if it's a boy?

Old Comrades

Talk these days
is of health concerns,
levels of medication,
cancer scares,
part-time employment,
no employment,
free bus passes,
the last funeral attended,
or the next commemoration.

Peace Time

"Reports are coming in."
Words that once paused all activity
and fingers turned radio dials
to full volume.

I hear those words today.
Now spoken by AA Roadwatch.
"An accident on the M50 at the Red Cow."
"A stray horse on the A28 outside Markethill."

The Conference

The conference was boring,
made even worse by atrocious acoustics,
though we clapped at the appropriate moments.

A hire car aided our escape
to a vineyard in the countryside;
an old castle where two Popes once stayed overnight.

Dusk was falling as we arrived
and the courtyard balustrades,
subtly illuminated,
created the sense of another world.

The wine-tasting was great
(I got double the quantity as you were driving)
and afterwards, we explored the castle.

In the small chapel you did not kneel,
nor genuflect,
but instead bent over the rear pew.

History

Walking on the beach
at the waters edge,
looking back to see
no trace
of my journey.
Footprints already washed away
with the latest wave.

How different our lives would be
if our past was wiped clean every few moments,
leaving only the present,
the now and the new,
and the anticipation
of what has yet to come.

Thirst

35 degrees in the mid-day sun.
The first mouthful of ice-cold beer
at the beach bar
never made it to my throat;
a parched tongue absorbed it
like a sponge.

Photo courtesy of Dara Mac Donaill

LAURENCE McKEOWN is an author, playwright, filmmaker, and academic though sees those roles within the broader context of political activism and the role that the arts can play in that.

His involvement in creative works, political education, and academia began during his period of incarceration as a political prisoner in the H-Blocks of Long Kesh (1976-1992). Following his release from prison Laurence completed a doctoral thesis at Queen's University, Belfast. His thesis was published in 2001 entitled *Out of Time*.

Whilst pursuing his PhD studies, Laurence co-wrote (with Brian Campbell) a feature film, *H3* (2001, Metropolitan Films), based on the 1981 hunger strike within the prison, which Laurence participated in (for 70 days) and during which 10 prisoners died.

In 1995 he co-founded the West Belfast Film Festival, which in 2001 expanded citywide to become the Belfast Film Festival. Laurence was chair of the film festival for its first ten years and remains on its board of management.

Laurence has written twelve plays, three books, one TV series, a radio drama, and three documentary films. His most recent play, *Green and Blue* (produced by Kabosh Theatre) was premiered at the Belfast International Arts Festival in 2016. It has toured Ireland extensively and been performed in Paris, Dresden, and London. Laurence was short-listed for the Irish Writers Guild of Ireland Zebbie Award (2017) for *Green and Blue*.

www.**salmon**poetry.com

"Like the sea-run Steelhead salmon that thrashes upstream to its spawning ground, then instead of dying, returns to the sea – Salmon Poetry Press brings precious cargo to both Ireland and America in the poetry it publishes, then carries that select work to its readership against incalculable odds."
Tess Gallagher